WOMEN OF Excellence

CREATION HOUSE

WOMEN OF *Excellence*

DELORES KENDRICK

Women of Excellence by Delores L. Kendrick
Published by Creation House
A Charisma Media Company
600 Rinehart Road
Lake Mary, Florida 32746
www.charismamedia.com

This book or parts thereof may not be reproduced in any form, stored in a retrieval system, or transmitted in any form by any means—electronic, mechanical, photocopy, recording, or otherwise—without prior written permission of the publisher, except as provided by United States of America copyright law.

Unless otherwise noted, all Scripture quotations are from the King James Version of the Bible.

Scripture quotations marked NIV are from the Holy Bible, New International Version of the Bible. Copyright © 1973, 1978, 1984, International Bible Society. Used by permission.

Scripture quotations marked NKJV are from the New King James Version of the Bible. Copyright © 1979, 1980, 1982 by Thomas Nelson, Inc., publishers. Used by permission.

Scripture quotations marked NLT are from the Holy Bible, New Living Translation, copyright © 1996, 2004, 2007 by Tyndale House Foundation. Used by permission of Tyndale House Publishers Inc., Carol Stream, Illinois, 60188. All rights reserved.

Design Director: Bill Johnson
Cover design by Nancy Panaccione

Copyright © 2012 by Delores L. Kendrick
All rights reserved.

Visit the author by e-mail: dl.kendrick@att.net

Library of Congress Cataloging-in-Publication Data:
2012948813
International Standard Book Number: 978-1-62136-313-2
E-book International Standard Book Number:
978-1-62136-314-9

While the author has made every effort to provide accurate telephone numbers and Internet addresses at the time of publication, neither the publisher nor the author assumes any responsibility for errors or for changes that occur after publication.

13 14 15 16 — 98765432
Printed in the United States of America

DEDICATION

First I thank the Lord Jesus Christ, the lover of my soul, for guiding me through the many experiences in my life. When I felt as though I could not make it and I was walking alone, He stood by my side and brought me through to victory.

This book is dedicated to my children, Sherrell, Debra, my granddaughter Eileen, and my church family.

ACKNOWLEDGMENTS

Sherrell and Debra, I want to thank you both for patiently encouraging me not only to finish this book, but for allowing me to share with others the calling of God on my life, and always working alongside me in the ministry. You have been gracious and kind when I have had to direct my attention to others rather than spend time with you.

Thank you, Eileen, for helping your grandmother and encouraging me in ways you will never know.

Thank you, Bernice, for encouraging me to finish this book, and for TOP, my church family, for your love and faithfulness to me.

I thank the Lord for my mother, who imparted into my life at an early age, and my father, who taught me that all things are possible if I will just believe.

TABLE OF CONTENTS

Introduction xiii

Chapter 1: Thank God for Josie................1

Chapter 2: Nothing Stays the Same 5

Chapter 3: Building on a Sure Foundation 13

Chapter 4: The Tabernacle of Moses 15

Chapter 5: A Garden Enclosed 19

Chapter 6: The Survival Technique 23

Chapter 7: Searching for Love In
All the Wrong Places........................27

Chapter 8: Just a Woman, or a Just Woman? 31

Chapter 9: Get Your House in Order............ 39

Chapter 10: Our Appearance
    Is Important to God 43

Chapter 11: Platform Ministry 47

Chapter 12: Dressing Appropriately
    for Ministry 53

Chapter 13: Tips for Ministry 61

Chapter 14: Women Who Turn Men Off 65

Chapter 15: Traveling Ministries 69

Chapter 16: Dinner Party Etiquette—
    What You Should Know 77

Chapter 17: Etiquette on the Cell Phone 83

Notes 87

About the Author 91

Contact the Author 93

INTRODUCTION

For more than thirty years I have observed women in leadership positions. I have admired their boldness and tenacity in pursuing their calling to platform ministry. Many women have accepted the fivefold office God has called them to with confidence and assurance that who God calls He will give audience. I have seen women who have a powerful charismatic flow that captivates the hearts of their audience as though they were held in a prison or state of complete mental absorption. The people were caught up in excitement and awe as they listened to the words of exhortation from the speaker. Not only was the presentation of the Word excellent, but also their appearance complemented their presentation.

Unfortunately I have noticed areas of change over the years that have disturbed me. There has been change in Christian ethics and character traits. I have seen a decline in the principles that those who have gone on before us had established as a foundation of excellence. I believe we are at the time and season where women must not only have the knowledge, charisma, and poise in their presentation, but also the character and integrity to accompany our gifting.

This book is for the women who may not have had the training that I was blessed to receive. It is for women of every culture, age, and ethnic background. My desire is that you will use this book as a tool and a guide to strive for excellence in your ministry, vocation, and everyday life.

CHAPTER 1

THANK GOD FOR JOSIE

I MUST GIVE HONOR and extended credit to my mother, who instilled in me the importance of living a life of excellence. Even though I was raised with three brothers, my mother was determined to make a lady out of me. My brothers were normal boys who climbed trees, shot bow and arrows, wrestled, had fistfights, and participated in many other activities that young boys do. I was the youngest and tagged along everywhere they went, trying to fit into a group of rough guys. I did pretty well; after all, I had to survive. However, my mother was always there to bring me into the house and let me know she was grooming me to become a lady. There were certain things necessary for me to learn—how ladies walk, talk, stand, and sit. Of course I did not like being sat down and pulled away from my brothers, but I am so grateful that she did not yield to my stubbornness.

I remember one Christmas my brother and I got new tennis shoes. His shoes were black and white and they were the higher top tennis shoes that only boys wore at that time. Girls wore a completely different style, and they were mostly pastel colors. Mother had bought me a white pair for Christmas. I was so upset because I wanted the same shoe style and color my brother had. Mother tried to talk sense to me. "Delores, you are a girl and they have different shoes for you than your brother." She explained to me that girls' tennis shoes are usually slimmer than boys' and have softer colors such as white, pink, and blue. I really did not care what girls were supposed to wear; I wanted shoes like my brother's. I remember walking through the house pouting and refusing to wear my new white tennis shoes.

After realizing no one was paying me any attention, and Mother was not going to change her mind, I reluctantly began to wear my white, low-cut slim tennis shoes made for little girls.

My mother was a very strict no-nonsense woman.

Once she said no, she would never go back on her word. I have learned to appreciate this quality, which she displayed throughout my childhood. I am by no means implying that she had all the answers, but the wisdom she had gained from observing others she applied in our home and later in my life. My mother did not finish high school, but she was blessed to be around those who mentored and instilled in her life certain virtues that made her a great example to me as well as others. She is now in paradise with her King, and one day I will go to her, what a reunion it will be.

CHAPTER 2

NOTHING STAYS THE SAME

W E ALL KNOW that nothing stays the same; life is about change. Looking back over the years, there have been many changes in the way things are done. Some of the changes are good, some are not. I want you to know I do embrace change; however, I believe some things should never change because they were established on the grounds of integrity and dignity. They are important and we must recognize the necessity and importance to never let them slip away from us. I am speaking of those little things that have been lost that characterized us as women of grace and women of excellence. I also must acknowledge that many women do not want to be seen in this fashion, so I respect your desires; but to those who wish to recapture the awesomeness of womanhood yet walk in the strength and authority of your calling, I address you.

As we look back in history we see where women were considered intellectually inferior to men, and also a major source of temptation, evil, and of the devil.

Women were always viewed as a creative source of human life, created yes, to be man's helpmeet; however, their main role was in conception. The resulting stereotype that "a woman's place is in the home" has largely determined the way in which women have expressed themselves. Today contraception, and in some areas legalized abortion, have given women greater control over the number of children they will bear.

Early Christian theology shared these views of St. Jerome, Latin father of the Christian church, who said, "Woman is the gate of the devil, the path of wickedness, the sting of the serpent."[1] In Greek mythology, it was a woman, Pandora, who opened the forbidden box and brought plagues and unhappiness to mankind. Early Roman Law described women as "children, forever inferior to men."[2]

The attitude toward women in the East was at

first positive. For example, in ancient India, women were not deprived of property rights and individual freedom of marriage, but Hinduism, which evolved in India after about 500 B.C., required women to be obedient toward men. Women had to walk behind their husbands. They also could not own property and widows could not remarry.[3]

In both the East and West, male children were preferred over female children. Nevertheless, when they were allowed personal and intellectual freedom, women made significant achievements. During the Middle Ages, nuns played key roles in European religious life. Aristocratic women enjoyed power and prestige. Whole areas were influenced by women rulers such as Queen Elizabeth of England in the sixteenth century, Catherine the Great of Russia in the eighteenth century, and Queen Victoria of England in the nineteenth century.[4]

Women were always considered weaker than men, unable to perform work that required muscular or intellectual development. Domestic chores were relegated to women in most preindustrial societies, leaving "heavier" labor to men. They ignored the fact that caring for children, washing clothes, and milking cows also required intensive labor. As a result, physiological tests now support that women have a greater tolerance to pain, and statistics reveal that women live longer and are more resistant to diseases.[5]

Traditionally, a middle class girl in Western

culture tended to learn from her mother's example that cooking, cleaning, and caring for the children were the behaviors expected of her when she grew up. Tests from the 1960s showed that academically, girls excelled more in the early grades than in high school, largely because the girl's own expectations declined because neither their families nor their teachers expected them to prepare for a future other than that of marriage and motherhood.[6] This trend has changed greatly in recent decades.

Formal education for girls historically has been secondary to that for boys. Girls could attend the master's schools for boys when there was room. By the end of the nineteenth century, the number of women students had increased greatly. Higher education particularly was broadened by the rise of women's colleges and the admission of women to regular colleges and universities. In 1870, an estimated one fifth of resident college and university students were women. By 1900 the proportion increased to more than one third.[7]

Women obtained 19 percent of all undergraduate college degrees around the beginning of the twentieth century. By 1984, the figure had greatly increased to 49 percent. Women also increased their numbers in graduate study. By the mid-1980s, women were earning 49 percent of all master's degrees and about 33 percent of all doctoral degrees. In 1985, about 53 percent of all college students were women, more than one quarter of whom were above age 29.[8]

In colonial America, women who earned their own living usually were seamstresses or kept boarding houses. But some women worked in professions and jobs available mostly to men. There were women doctors, lawyers, preachers, teachers, writers, and singers. By the early nineteenth century, however, acceptable occupations for working women were limited to factory labor or domestic work. Women were excluded from the professions, except for writing and teaching.[9]

The medical profession is an example of changed attitudes in the nineteenth and twentieth centuries about what was regarded as suitable work for women. Prior to the 1800s there were almost no medical schools, and virtually any enterprising person could practice medicine. Indeed, obstetrics was the domain of women.[10]

In 1890, women constituted about 5 percent of the total doctors in the United States. During the 1980s, the proportion was about 17 percent. At the same time, the percentage of women doctors was about 19 percent in West Germany and 20 percent in France. In Israel, however, about 32 percent of the total number of doctors and dentists were women.[11]

Over time, women improved their status in other professions. In 1930, about 2 percent of all American lawyers and judges were women. In 1989, about 22 percent. In 1930, there were almost no women engineers in the United States. In 1989, the proportion of women engineers was only 7.5 percent. In 2005, 92 percent of registered nurses, 82 percent of all elementary and middle school teachers, and 98 percent of all preschool and kindergarten teachers were women. In comparison, only 13 percent of all civil engineers, 7 percent of electrical and electronics engineers, and 3 percent of all aircraft pilots and flight engineers were female.[12]

Women are also obtaining advanced degrees and becoming more successful in the workplace. According to the current population survey conducted by the Bureau of Labor Statistics, women made up 46.7 percent of the labor force in 2009, and 51.4 percent of those women comprised professional and managerial positions.[13]

According to the United States Department of Labor Women's Bureau:

- In 2010 of the 123 million women ages sixteen years and over in the US, 72 million, or 58.6 percent, were labor force participants—working or looking for work.
- Women comprised 47 percent of the total US labor force.
- Women are projected to account for 51 percent of the increase in total labor force growth between 2008 and 2018.
- Sixty-six million women were employed in the US—73 percent of employed

women worked on full-time jobs, while 27 percent worked on a part-time basis.

- The largest percentage of employed women (40.6 percent) worked in management, professional, and related occupations; 32.0 percent worked in sales and office occupations; 21.3 percent in service occupations; 5.2 percent in production, transportation, and material moving occupations; and 0.9 percent in natural resources, construction, and maintenance occupations.[14]

Women today are in positions of greater power and authority in a wider variety of fields than ever before. Ladies, we have come a long way.

CHAPTER 3

BUILDING ON A SURE FOUNDATION

For no one can lay any foundation other than the one already laid, which is Jesus Christ.
—1 Corinthians 3:11, niv

WHEN AN ARCHITECT designs a building, he concentrates on the foundation; the higher the skyscraper, the stronger the foundation. The building will not stand without a firm foundation.

He can build on a shaky foundation, one that is not deep enough, and have beautiful rooms and furnishings, but if that foundation is not right, it will eventually fall.

Foundations are the most important and crucial aspects in building anything. When building a house, foundations and residential footings are crucial to the success of a building. Footings and foundations, when properly designed and constructed, withstand all the forces of a house and the powerful forces of nature. When we look at the outward structure and design of many of our modern buildings today, we fail sometimes to see the hidden technology for which the building stands. So it is in the spiritual realm.

CHAPTER 4

THE TABERNACLE OF MOSES

Make this tabernacle and all its furnishings exactly like the pattern I will show you.
—Exodus 25:9, NIV

As we look at the tabernacle of Moses described in the Book of Exodus, we see an awesome example of a temple of excellence. The architect was God Himself, the mastermind of builders. God spared no cost and time to its construction. Every detail, every piece of material and all furnishings were relevant, because it was here that God chose to dwell and communicate with His people. At the completion of the tabernacle, Moses had to inspect it to see if it measured up to and met the specification that God Himself had instructed.

The furnishings in the tabernacle were constructed by divine design. I believe the tabernacle of Moses gives an example of how God wants to see His church. It was designed by God because He could not leave the construction to the hand of man. The tabernacle had to be a place where God met with man, the place where the people would come to worship, and where the people would give the glory to God (Exod. 25–27). God wants to place within us the furnishings that represent and demonstrate the character and attributes of the divine nature of Christ. The spiritual body of Christ would be a temple of sacrifice, transparency, righteousness, fruitfulness, and healing both emotionally and physically. The excellence of Christ would be manifested as we stood before the people, thus bringing glory to His great name.

The materials used to build the tabernacle are a symbol of the great value of the Lord Jesus Christ. God wanted to instill in the minds and hearts of the people that when they looked at the tabernacle they would see the spiritual truths. The valuable metals and beautiful colors would be a symbol of the majesty and beauty of our Lord Jesus Christ.

God wants to tabernacle within us and place the furnishings in their proper place so we will show forth His love and beauty. He wants the graces that release the sweet aroma of Christ to flow from us to a world that needs to see and experience the reality of who Christ really is.

CHAPTER 5

A GARDEN ENCLOSED

A garden enclosed Is my sister, my spouse,
A spring shut up, A fountain sealed.
—Song of Solomon 4:12, nkjv

Ladies, we must seek not only to be anointed in our delivery of the Word of God, but also seek to possess the integrity and character that will cause the world to desire a true and living Christ. I have found that if God anoints anything it will be His Word, even if it comes out of the mouth of a donkey or rooster. As God's chosen vessels you have been given the freedom and honor to share the Word of God with the world. I do not feel we have yet tapped into the level of anointing that our heavenly Father wants to bestow upon us. I believe there is a woman inside waiting to come forth, a woman who is healed emotionally as well as physically. There is a woman who has discovered her identity at the foot of the cross, and is ready to be all God wants her to be. She does not have to imitate or mimic anyone. She has found her identity in Christ, and has accepted who she is. She is comfortable in her womanhood and does not have to impress anyone by placing a mask over her emotions and becoming something she is not in order to be accepted. She has discovered who she is, and when she stands before the masses she can be just that—a woman of excellence.

The foundation on which we build must be Jesus Christ. All other ground is shaky and unstable. If our foundation is faulty, the whole building will be worthless because it will not stand the pressures that will eventually come against it (Matt. 7:24–29). The tabernacle of Moses gives us an example of excellence and how we should make sure we are solid in our foundation, so when we begin to build, it will stand against any opposition, any crisis, or any persecution that we must all conquer in our lives.

When you have a strong foundation, the obstacles that we face in our lives serve as a platform to propel us to the next level. If we focus on these crises we will be distracted from the purpose they were meant to fulfill in our lives at that particular time. We must learn to stand when we have built on the right foundation. Our attitude will be pleasing and demonstrate the beauty of Christ. No matter how we try to hide our emotions, if there is any unhealed area it will be manifested in our speech and behavior, because what is within us will be seen outwardly. The foundation of a thing will always determine its greatness.

CHAPTER 6

THE SURVIVAL TECHNIQUE

My child, pay attention to what I say. Listen carefully to my words. Don't lose sight of them. Let them penetrate deep into your heart, for they bring life to those who find them, and healing to their whole body.
—PROVERBS 4:20–22, NLT

THERE ARE FEW if any in this life who have not experienced and suffered some dysfunction in their childhood or adulthood. We live in an imperfect world. We learn how to survive, so we become experts in concealing our true feelings. It is a survival technique that we have mastered. We learn to live with pain and push it so far in the back of our minds that we deceive ourselves into believing many things did not even happen in our lives. We have become experts in hiding our true feelings because we do not know what exactly will come out of us if we just let go.

People say, "keep it real," but then you hear that you are supposed to smile when you don't feel like it. So which is better, showing your true emotions or hiding them? I do not feel we are hiding our emotions. I do believe deception is at play here. We do not realize that the pain we have carried and buried deep within us has caused us to be in denial of its very existence. However, whatever is within you will come out one way or another, whether it is in your communication, your relationships, or in your presentation to your audiences. Many people have confronted me over the years with the question, "Why do I get angry for no reason at all? I find myself being very sharp and abrupt when there is no reason to be," or they will say, "When I see this person I get annoyed or uncomfortable."

As we look back on our childhood we have sweet

memories of the holidays. The smells of turkey and dressing at Thanksgiving and baking cookies at Christmas bring precious thoughts of fun laughter. Not all memories are sweet and joyful, though. Some have experienced emotional pain remembering the holidays or certain celebrated or non-celebrated events in their past.

Some women have gone to their physician because certain smells cause emotional reactions of discomfort and even anger. They attribute these symptoms to allergies, when many times it is the pain that has taken place in their lives due to their bitter past. When you first smell a new scent you link it to an event, a person, a thing, or even a moment. Your brain forges a link between the smell and a memory. Smells often call up childhood memories, many of which are not pleasant. If we are not healed in our emotions we can be affected later in our lives.

In her article, "How Smell Works," Sarah Dowdey states, "A smell can bring on a flood of memories, influence people's moods and even affect their work performance. Because the olfactory bulb is part of the brain's limbic system, an area so closely associated with memory and feeling it's sometimes called the 'emotional brain,' smell can call up memories and powerful responses almost instantaneously."[1]

Unfortunately, many have been in denial for so long or have used the survival technique of burying the pain so deep in their consciousness that they do not know why they react or respond the way they do. The Holy Spirit wants to heal those deep wounds that have controlled their lives and prevented so many women from experiencing the freedom to be who they were created to be. The Holy Spirit wants to remove the words that are so common to many, "That's just the way I am," from your vocabulary. That is why I feel an understanding of the tabernacle of Moses is so vital in our lives today.

CHAPTER 7

SEARCHING FOR LOVE IN ALL THE WRONG PLACES

For the woman at the well in John 4:1–42, Jesus restored her true identity and directed her to fulfill her destiny, her God-given purpose in life. Remember the first thing He said to her, it was in the form of a command, "Give Me water"?

Jesus knew that she had deep within her a capacity to love, but her garden had been sealed up and in its place she had built a wall of protection where there was no trust. Therefore she only looked for someone to fulfill her natural, fleshly need. She had no idea the worth and beauty that was hidden within the confines of the walls surrounding her life.

When Jesus first addressed her, His words were directed to the very thing she was to do in life. Give water to the thirsty soul. Give food to the hungry. Someone is hurting out in this world that needs what you have to give. Someone is looking for fulfillment in the various appetites that their flesh offers them, which is temporal.

"Give Me water" is a command, not a question. In other words, when you first minister to my need, then you will be able to minister to the world. The answer was in worshiping the Lord. Your first priority is in Christ. Christ was saying, "Meet My need first. I am God and I created you to worship Me. You did not choose Me, but I chose you before the foundation of the world that you would be worship unto Me." When you give a libation offering to the Lord, which is an emptying of your very soul, pouring out all the bitterness and disappointments of your past, until you are totally free from carrying all that pain that has weighted you down for so many years, you will be ready to be filled with His love and grace. You will then find your identity and see the beauty of who you really are.

Like this woman, you must learn how to draw

from that deep well of your very soul, and release from deep within all the pain, frustration, anxiety, loneliness, and disappointments in your life. You have been disappointed and deceived from the men in your life. Disappointments on the job have caused you to feel inadequate and you have given up your dream. There has been no fulfillment, no change, because what you are looking for, man does not have it to give.

You are looking for love in all the wrong places, yet your love is not pure. For it is full of all life's sorrows and woes. Therefore you are getting back that which you are giving, wounded spirit, a heart full of pain.

CHAPTER 8

JUST A WOMAN, OR A JUST WOMAN?

THERE ARE THOSE who have sat in the pews of the congregation, sitting at their desk in their offices wondering what is going on inside of me? They have become uncomfortable, and restless in their spirit. Feeling as though, I know there is something greater for me in this life. Many do not realize they are getting ready to break forth out of their shells of false security and step into the waters of faith to become the woman God ordained them to be. I believe many couples shall emerge and flow together, and many singles will accept their call for singleness for this season in their lives. No, you are not just a woman, but you are a Just, Pure Woman, raised up for such a time as this.

The church is going through a great time of cleansing and purging, so we can come into the new dimension that is coming forth in this hour The Holy Spirit is preparing His people. Out of this preparation of cleansing will come forth a company of women, who are righteous, going forth with kingdom principles, and ready to make a people ready for the coming of the King.

"Many daughters have done virtuously, but thou excellest them all" (Prov. 31:29). When we look up the word *virtuous*, it means, honest, respectful, pure, untarnished, descent, unspotted, chaste, clean, sexually innocent, guiltless, upright, walk a straight path.

Honesty seems to be a thing of the past today. Saints can look in your eyes and lie without blinking an eye. Respect, what is that? People can come into the church, lift their hands and praise God, speak in some kind of tongue and go home to their arranged relationship, and share how good the service was.

The word *upright* means to walk a straight path, not to the right or the left. "If we say we have fellowship with Him and walk in darkness, we lie and do not the truth" (1 John 1:6). This woman described in Proverbs 31 is pure, respectful, and just, not a woman with a lot of issues and hang-ups; certainly not an angry woman because of her experiences of the past.

Our Lord upon His return is coming back for a church that is pure, honest, full-grown, ripe, not one that is undeveloped. He is looking for someone in this hour He can impregnate and trust with His purposes; someone who will carry them until the time of birthing. One strong enough to carry His purposes, regardless of the circumstance or the environment they find themselves in. You might get a little nauseated you may stumble at times but you will not abort the seed of purpose, because what you are pregnant with is what you are going to birth.

Many women today are pregnant with many things! Their own success, their own fame, their own beauty. Ezekiel 16:15 says, "But thou didst trust in thine own beauty, and playedst the harlot because of thy renown, and pouredst out thy fornications on every one that passed by; his it was." In other words anyone who would open their doors unto you, they were allowed in.

You got wrapped up in you. You started having intimacy with yourself, your own thing; you conceived your own desires, your own vision, and you birthed out you.

Proverbs 31:29 tells us, "Many daughters have done virtuously, but you excellest them all." What could this woman do to excel all of these qualities, which are described as virtuous? As I thought on this, the

Holy Spirit brought my attention to two words in the verse: *have done*.

Webster's Dictionary says the word *have* is an auxiliary verb used with a past participle to form perfect tenses, to cease, finish, become weary of or disgusted with whatever has been done. "Many daughters have done virtuously..." Somewhere along the journey they lost something. Many women have become weary—"I have had it!" Disgusted, tired, terminated—I have concluded. Many women have worn out, become used up. But you, daughter, are a ripe, fertile, full blossom, because you have not stopped. Then I looked up the word *excel*, and *Webster's Dictionary* said to be over and above, surpassing, expert, consultant, sharp, no slouch, skilled workman. To shine in, to be born for. You, yes, have done virtuously, and you are yet doing virtuously. For this, you have excelled them all.

We never come to a place of completion until the race is finished. Galatians 5:7 says, "You were running a good race. Who cut in on you and kept you from obeying the truth?" You have done all of these things. But, what you are doing now, determines the level of your excellence.

Seasoning means maturity. Qualified, it takes time for seasoning to penetrate our food, it takes process of the fire, heat for the seasonings to go into food to enhance the flavor. You cannot cook too fast, it is a slow process. Likewise the fire brings out the fragrance of the believer when we go through our trials and test.

In the tabernacle of Moses, the spices were prepared and poured on the altar for God's consumption. The continual flow of spices upon the altar is what makes the vessel of excellence. It is a continual pouring out, never ending.

What makes the bride of Christ excel them all? This is not something that is a quick fix. This is a continual work within of the spices spoken of in the tabernacle of Moses. You might say what really does this have to do with me?

The ingredients of the incense points to the various aspects of ministry to God. The incense was composed of four "sweet spices," in equal proportion blended (salted) together. The incense was to be offered morning and evening upon the golden altar, upon the coals of fire taken from the altar of burnt offering.

The coals from one to another show the intimacy, and how they were linked together. All the fragrances had to be crushed and balanced. Through the making of the precious spices we not only see Christ but we must see also ourselves as we are being made the righteous of Christ. We can be that virtuous woman which excels above all.

First it was the precious Galbanum, a sap of resinous gum which came from a tree and received its origin from the combination from two plants. By itself it has a bitter, disagreeable taste that was used to drive away insects, reptiles, rats, and other pests. Yet it was used as a medicine. It lost its identity by being crushed very fine.

> For he shall grow up before him as a tender plant, and as a root out of a dry ground: he hath no form nor comeliness; and when we shall see him, there is no beauty that we should desire him. He is despised and rejected of men; a man of sorrows, and acquainted with grief: and we hid as it were our faces from him; he was despised, and we esteemed him not.
> —ISAIAH 53:2–3

Second, stacte (Greek). The Hebrew word is *nataph*, meaning "to drop," "distil," so called from the drops of gum which come from the tree producing it. It is also translated "balm." The word is used for rain, as in:

> Listen, O heavens, and I will speak; hear, O earth, the words of my mouth. Let my teaching fall like rain, and my words descend like dew, like showers on new grass, like abundant rain on tender plants. O LORD, when you went out from Seir, when you marched from the land of Edom, the earth shook, the heavens poured, the clouds poured down water. (RAIN)
> —DEUTERONOMY 32:1–2

Similar to this it is used describing the speech as flowing forth or distilling: "My speech dropped upon them: and the water for me as for the rain."

Third, Onycha, a ground shell fish taken from the sea; a Greek word meaning literally a "finger nail." It received its fragrance from what it ate. It was said it fed on the "nard" or stems of fragrant plants by the water, which reminds us that Christ fed not on the flesh pots of Egypt but on the will of His Father.

Also, if ground fine, it could be used as a medicine, and when burned, gives a pleasing perfume.

> Jesus answered, "It is written: 'Man does not live on bread alone, but on every word that comes from the mouth of God.'"
> —Matthew 4:4

Frankincense is white. A pure white gum which burns with a white flame. It has a bitter taste, and when it is ignited it burns freely. Note: this gum is obtained by an incision in a tree. It is used for medicine and is an antidote for poisons.

Notice all the spices have healing qualities. The anointing in Praise and Worship brings deliverance. When Praise ascends unto God from our spirit, soul, and body, it will bring health to us. Each balanced the other.

Ladies, we balance one another. In ministry unto God we are the spices that bring the fragrance together. Remember, some of the spices received their fragrance from what they ate. We must eat of the Word of God, and allow it to go to all parts of spirit, soul, and body and bring the wholeness needed to become all that He desires us to be. The spices were balanced; we want to balance in our walk with the Lord. Allow the Holy Spirit to pour Himself into your lives, until we see transformation take place each and every day of our lives.

CHAPTER 9

GET YOUR HOUSE IN ORDER

Let all things be done decently and in order.
—1 Corinthians 14:40

Looking again at the furnishings in the tabernacle, which are symbolic of the furnishings within the believer's life, we have a beautiful picture of the church. Every piece of furniture had to be in proper order. This was set by the divine order of God. As Moses was instructed to place the articles in their proper place, so it is with our lives. I strongly believe the Holy Spirit is calling us to get our house in order. For where there is no order there will be disorder. This holds true with our natural houses as well as our spiritual house.

When your home does not have order, frustration comes. You cannot find anything because everything is out of place. Nothing is working right. This causes you to miss appointments and be late to your place of employment, adding stress to your already stressful life.

I remember I was in between flights at the airport. I thought I would find a restroom close by my gate, as I hate to use the restrooms on the plane. They were just about getting ready to announce the passengers who needed help to board, so I had plenty of time; also, the flight was full. I went to the restroom, which was very close—only when I got there a sign was on the door: "Out of Order." I am sure you can imagine my frustration.

Have you been in a hurry to get to a meeting, only to get caught in a traffic jam? You reach the place of meeting, which is on the third or fourth floor, and the elevator is out of order. Carrying your briefcase, you run to find the stairway and proceed up the stairs, all the time scolding yourself for not continuing the exercise classes you joined two years ago and never attended.

Yes, when things are not in order they add stress

to our lives. There are some things we have no control of; however, there are many things we can control, but it takes work. We must set priorities in our lives and work to maintain them, and keep them in the order of importance.

God has called women to be the vessels in which His presence abides. He desires for us to become the gold that depicts our Lord and Savior Jesus Christ.

There are areas in our lives I believe God would desire us to pay special attention to. What may seem insignificant to us might be the very thing God wants to address in our lives. It may be the very thing that prevents us from fulfilling the destiny to which we are called. These are the areas I will address at this time, using the tabernacle of Moses as a guide.

God spoke to Moses and gave him divine instructions for the building of His tabernacle, which was set in the wilderness. This was the place where God would dwell on earth. This is where He would communicate with the priest and give instruction to Israel. This was the place where God would receive the offerings from Israel. There had to be divine order in the worship to Yahweh.

There were the metals of gold, silver, bronze, and brass, the colors of purple, scarlet, white, and blue. The fine linen all made up the beauty that was designed by God for the tabernacle of Moses. Every piece of furniture in the tabernacle was significant to the life of the believer. Every bolt, bar, ring, hook, and board, no matter how small, was necessary for the priest to function and carry out the divine will of God.

Scripture tells us we are the sanctuary that Christ dwells in. We must keep it clean and all the furnishings within us must be kept in the order that pleases our God.

> And also the burnt offerings were in abundance, with the fat of the peace offerings, and the drink offerings for every burnt offering. So the service of the house of the LORD was set in order.
> —2 CHRONICLES 29:35

CHAPTER 10

OUR APPEARANCE IS IMPORTANT TO GOD

What? Know ye not that your body is the temple of the Holy Ghost which is in you, which ye have of God, and ye are not your own?
—1 Corinthians 6:19

WE HAVE THE awesome privilege of showing off Christ to the world, not only when we are speaking, but in our character, appearance, and our everyday life.

As leaders our appearance is very important. The first thing one sees when we grace the platform is really what we look like—what we have on, how we walk, tall or short, the color of our skin, our hair, and so forth. People form a first impression based on what they see. It takes just a quick glance, maybe three or four seconds, for someone to evaluate you when you first walk out on a platform or meet for the first time. In this short time, the other person forms an opinion about you based on your appearance, your body language, your demeanor, your mannerisms, and how you are dressed.

Of course physical appearance matters. The person or people you are making your presentation to may not have ever seen you and your appearance is usually the first clue on how they will perceive you. But it certainly does not mean you need to look like a model to create a strong and positive first impression. No, the key to a good impression is to present yourself appropriately.

They say a picture is worth a thousand words, and so the "picture" you first present says much about you to the person you are meeting. Is your appearance saying the right things to help create the right impression? In *The New Professional Image*, authors Susan

Bixler and Nancy Nix-Rice said, "Books are judged by their covers, houses are appraised by their curb appeal, and people are initially evaluated on how they choose to dress and behave. In a perfect world this is not fair, moral, or just. What's inside should count a great deal more. Eventually it usually does, but not right away."[1]

In his article "Appearance Is Important," Stephen Boyd said, "Remember that your presentation begins the moment someone recognizes you as the speaker. This might be in the elevator, the restroom, or even in the parking garage. As soon as you are in close proximity to your speaking location, act as though you are on stage—because you may be."[2]

CHAPTER 11

PLATFORM MINISTRY

When we are on a platform, whether we are standing or sitting, all eyes are upon us. We are sending a message to our audience that this is the way you are to present yourselves before an audience. This is the reason we work at looking our best. And while this is very important, we must equally work on our character. Sometimes we spend much time on the outward appearance, not realizing the inner man that no one sees reflects the outward. Who we are inward will always be seen in our speech.

Our speech must be seasoned with salt in order for us to flow in love, power, and victory rather than defeat.

Colossians 4:5-6 tells us to "Walk in wisdom toward them that are without, redeeming the time. Let your speech be always with grace, seasoned with salt, that ye may know how ye ought to answer every man."

Salt is essential for the Christian. One of the things it represents is our speech. According to Wikipedia, "The role of salt in the Bible is relevant to understanding Hebrew society during the Old Testament and New Testament periods. Salt is a necessity of life and was a mineral that was used since ancient times in many cultures as a seasoning, a preservative, a disinfectant, a component of ceremonial offerings, and as a unit of exchange."[1]

For those of us who cook, we know that recipes always call for salt even it is a pinch. This seasoning has the power to pull all the other seasonings together and enhances and completes the recipe. The scripture tells us we are the salt of the earth. Our speech can turn away wrath and bring peace to unpleasant situations (Prov. 15:1).

In Leviticus 2:13, God commanded that "every oblation of thy meat offering shalt thou season with salt; neither shalt thou suffer the salt of the covenant of thy God to be lacking from thy meat offering: with all thine offerings thou shalt offer salt."

Jesus calls His disciples (and perhaps the crowds listening to the Sermon on the Mount), "the salt of the earth." He may be exhorting them to usefulness, or to fidelity, or referring to their role in purifying the world.

We want to be salted so our speech seasons those we minister to with grace and healing. Ladies, if we have not been healed of our bitter past, it will be reflected in our presentation before the audience.

If we have not dealt with anger, unforgiveness, guilt, jealousy, intimidation, or insecurities it will eventually surface. Circumstances in our lives will bring it up. The little cutting tones, the negative and sarcastic remarks in our speech will continue to pop up.

Many times as I work on my laptop at my office I get those pop-ups, which can really be annoying. I can continue to close them, but that will not get rid of them on a permanent basis. I may have to get pop-up removal software to remove it permanently in order to gain control of my work. What am I saying? Those little areas of our lives where certain incidents continue to pop up become annoying because they affect our lives, and we become distracted and many times lose control. They affect our lives in such a forceful way that we cannot communicate the graces of the Christ within. They rob us of our true identity.

The inappropriate little sarcastic jokes we use in a clandestine manner—these are hindrances in our lives that will prevent us from being as effective in the lives of those who make up our audience. While speaking many times I have seen those who have come across angry and harsh in making their point without realizing it. They have taken on a different personality, which comes from the pain that has been imbedded inside, and they have been in denial for many years.

Women who have suffered rejection whether from men or women must make sure you have received the healing needed. Many times we see the rejection in the way you come across on the platform or in communicating to others. As women you do not have to portray masculinity to prove you can preach or flow in the Holy Spirit. The anointing is not in your genes but in the Christ. The anointing is not in the volume of your voice but in the Holy Spirit. I am not saying you cannot be demonstrative, I am just saying you must be who you are, whether you are a demonstrative individual or a quiet one. Don't allow others to dictate to you who you are. Do not look for someone to validate your calling. Christ has already called and confirmed your calling to whatever area of ministry you have been called to. Be free to be you, for you are the one God will anoint.

Remember I shared about those little pop-ups that become annoying? God has equipped and called Holy Ghost-filled counselors who know how to minister and walk you through deliverance in those weak areas of your lives. You do not have to carry the pain of your bitter past. You can be healed, where you no longer have to deal with those pop-ups; you can be free to be who you really are. You can meet for the first time the real you. Don't let pride stop you from being all God has called you to be.

CHAPTER 12

DRESSING APPROPRIATELY FOR MINISTRY

Wear clothing suitable for the audience you are speaking to. If you are not sure, ask the program planner when you are learning about your audience. When possible, dress one notch up from the audience.

Do not wear clothing that can be distracting; your

appearance should blend in well with your content and the audience to which you are speaking.

I remember years ago when I was going to a meeting and that night I had to speak. When the plane landed my luggage was not there. I was wearing jeans and a sweater. I quickly went to the hotel and purchased a white shirt and borrowed a beautiful scarf, changed my jewelry (because I always travel with my jewelry), and went to the meeting. It worked. However, from that time on I always made sure I carried a change of clothing that would be appropriate in any setting.

Ladies, do not be stingy with the cost; it will pay off when you look in the mirror. Remember the tabernacle of Moses? As you study the furnishings that were placed in the courts you will be amazed when you see the costly materials God commanded the priest to use:

> The LORD said to Moses, "Tell the Israelites to bring me an offering. You are to receive the offering for me from each man whose heart prompts him to give. These are the offerings you are to receive from them: gold, silver and bronze; blue, purple and scarlet yarn and fine linen; goat hair; ram skins dyed red and hides of sea cows; acacia wood; olive oil for the light; spices for the anointing oil and for the fragrant incense; and onyx stones and other gems to be mounted on the ephod and breastpiece. Then have them make a sanctuary for me, and I will

dwell among them. Make this tabernacle and all its furnishings exactly like the pattern I will show you."

—Exodus 25:1–8, NIV

I know we live in a church age where many things have changed concerning the attire we wear; however, I still believe we are the New Testament priest of the Lord and we represent the most high God. We must look our best whether we have a suit or jeans, heels or sandals. Of course, you can purchase the most expensive knit, the most beautiful dress, or the most gorgeous slacks, but if your foundation is not together, you will not shine on the outside. This works spiritually as well as naturally.

FOUNDATIONS

We talked about the spiritual foundation, now I would like to speak about our natural foundation. There was a time when girdles (shapers) were not very comfortable. We felt confined and it was difficult to breathe. Well, time has brought many changes, and there are many selections that are very comfortable.

There is a reason why we wear girdles. It is to hold those parts of the body in place so we will not shift from side to side. That may seem comical; however, it is not very comical when you are walking back and forth on a platform in front of a large crowd of people, and it certainly is not very attractive.

When we reach a certain age many times we acquire that extra body fat around our midriff, causing our clothing to not have a smooth finish. Your department store has an area that deals specifically in foundations. The sales person can help you in your selection if you do not know the proper foundation to purchase. Many women say they do not like the way they feel in girdles; however, there are many different styles today that are very comfortable. As a matter of fact, they do not even refer to them as girdles but shapers. If you select the right one for you it can be very comfortable and flattering to the figure.

Looking at this from a spiritual view, the apostle Paul while observing a Roman soldier had a powerful revelation on the armor of God. One of the pieces of armor was the girdle. This girdle, called the "girdle of truth," was connected to the breastplate and it held the weapons of war in it (Eph. 6:14). Truth must be braced tightly around the loins of the mind so the believer would not be moved about with every wind of doctrine. This is vital to the Christian life.

Whether ministering to thousands or sitting in the audience, you do not want people concentrating on any one part of your body. Ladies, we do not want to draw attention to an area of our body that is not properly groomed. Your foundation will give you a smooth finish to your apparel, and cause your outer garments to look nice. Remember it starts with the foundation.

Connected to the girdle was the breastplate of

righteousness. This brings me to the next piece of clothing that is very important.

THE BRA

As we walk back and forth across the platform, nothing looks more distasteful than to see a woman who is wearing the improper size or the wrong type of bra for her figure. It is important to be properly fitted so you are not showing cleavage or oozing out of your bra, causing your outer garment to bulge.

If you are a full-figured woman or if you have a problem sizing, I would suggest a long line bra that will pull in your midriff causing your clothes to fit very smooth. You may feel that you will be confined and uncomfortable, but as I said, there is a perfect fit for you if you will receive help from a salesperson who specializes in fitting you properly.

I realize we are in a time in the fashion world where it is popular to wear bras that reveal a lot of cleavage. Ladies, we are in the world but we are not of the world. I do not believe it is necessary to go to the extreme and wear clothing up to our necks; there is balance where we can be stylish and yet fashionable. Women, we can be attractive in our apparel and be the Esthers God is calling for in this hour.

KNITS

Knits have always been very sophisticated and comfortable. Traveling can be a headache with all the guidelines and restrictions we have enforced upon us today. I have found that knits work. They pack tight in the luggage and they do not wrinkle if packed correctly. I have found rolling each piece separately keeps most of the wrinkles out. When purchasing your knits be sure to have them blocked. A good knit will always block to your body size. You do not want it to be too tight but fit smooth over every part of your body. This will give you a smooth look to the hip area and other parts of your body. Again, as a rule the sales person will block your knit free of charge.

DRESS LENGTH

Wear your dress length appropriate for sitting and bending. Many times as we pray for those at the altar we find ourselves in positions that can be revealing. As stated earlier, exposing cleavage is often seen in women's ministry. Women, let us be more modest in our dress.

Avoid wearing your clothes too tight, make sure you have room in your clothes to move about and be comfortable. Remember we are not in a fashion show. The clothing we wear may be suitable for attending a particular function but not appropriate for ministering.

Yet, we must always be prepared, for we never know when we will be called on unexpectedly.

Ladies, when wearing a dress or skirt, sit with your legs crossed at the ankles. This is comfortable and it looks nice.

FRAGRANCE

Women, please do not spray too much perfume on, especially when ministering, as there are many people who have allergies. Also, too much perfume interferes with ministry at the altar. I very seldom wear perfume when ministering, but I will wear a mild lotion of my choice, which still gives a fragrance that is not overpowering.

Let's remember that perfumes do not take the place of a good shower and deodorant. Many women perspire more than others while under a heavy anointing. Find the right deodorant for you, and if you need assistance your doctor will help you select the right one.

CHAPTER 13

TIPS FOR MINISTRY

I REMEMBER I WAS in a city ministering at the altar. A young lady fell on my shoulder and when she finally released me I was wearing half of her makeup. Lipstick and makeup was all over my suit, and it was ruined. The cleaners were never able to remove all of the stains. That is why I place a cloth on my shoulder many times when ministering deliverance as to save my clothing. It works.

Many times when ministering, because of close contact with the people their makeup can easily come off on your clothes. Yet you do not want to stop ministering in this way, and you do not want the person to be hurt when they find out they have gotten makeup on your clothes.

I have always shared with women to brush their teeth, because we as ministers do not want to offend others with bad breath. Select a good mouthwash and gargle deep. Be sure to brush your tongue and make regular appointments with your dentist. Bad breath many times comes from teeth that need attending and the food you eat. Mints do not take the place of caring for your teeth.

You must be careful what you eat before ministry, as too much spicy food can cause offensive breath. Train yourself to drink plenty of water. This was a very difficult thing for me to discipline myself to, because I did not like the taste of water. I was told by a minister friend that I must drink water if I was going to stay healthy as I traveled in the work of the Lord. I began to pray and discipline myself to drink water even though I did not like it. Over the years I have developed a taste for water and I really love it.

Medical doctors will tell you water makes up more than two thirds of human body weight, and without water, we would die in a few days. The human brain is made up of 95 percent water, blood is 82 percent and lungs 90 percent. An estimated 75 percent of Americans have mild, chronic dehydration.[1]

Remember, our body is the temple of God; we must

keep it holy. This is done by putting in your body and on your body those things that will glorify our Lord.

Gum Chewing

Please do not chew gum. We often see this with musicians, and it doesn't look very nice.

Cell Phones

Cell phones have gotten out of hand. Please put them on vibrate when in public places. I think it is rude to be speaking on your cell phone in church while service is going on, and yet we see this all the time.

CHAPTER 14

WOMEN WHO TURN MEN OFF

WOMEN HAVE ASKED me over the years why men brush them off in ministry. They feel that men do not respect their call to ministry. I would like to address this issue. There could be many reasons. One reason could be the religious thinking and background as mentioned in the beginning of this book.

Another reason could be the way women present themselves. Women, we must remember and never forget we are ladies, not men. We do not have to use the body language that men use, and we can be the feminine ladies we were meant to be, as we have already addressed in the previous chapter. When you know who you are, versus what you do, you will fulfill the purpose for your life with dignity.

Sometimes we want those from the male gender to accept our calling, and we feel we must imitate them to be approved. I do not get the idea of Jesus preaching on the mount yelling in anger and an organ backing Him. Let me be clear; I am not criticizing this flow of ministry if this is the real you. But many women feel if they do not preach like a man, they will not be accepted as ministering in the anointing. This is not true. You must know who you are, versus what and how you do a thing. Ladies, if this is the real you, then by all means please do not change. I have some women friends in ministry that preach under the anointing in such a dynamic way. You can hardly sit in your seat when they are preaching—in fact, I don't. So, I am not saying you have to act timid and you cannot be loud. There are times the anointing comes upon me and my voice rises in a crescendo. All I am saying is do not lose your identity. Be who you are and be the best of you.

There is nothing more beautiful than a woman being a woman. I want you to recognize the beauty in being you. No one can be a better you than you. God will anoint the real you, not the person you try to be.

When you know and accept how God has made you, you will realize you are one of a kind.

I feel another turnoff from pastors is when you have been invited to speak to their congregation and you come in with the attitude to change their way of worship. When you come into another assembly you are now under the authority of the leadership of that particular church regardless of your office. And you should conduct yourself in the grace and integrity of the Holy Spirit. True, we have been given revelation, but wisdom gives direction of when and where to give that revelation you have received. I have received revelations on a particular area that I could not share for six and seven years. This is for men as well as women. If you are not wise, you can cause a pastor much more work than necessary, as he will have to try to put his church back together after a zealous immature ministry has brought confusion to his congregation.

I received a call a few years ago from a young evangelist calling himself a prophet. He called asking for help because he was stranded in a city where he had been invited to minister. After the first night the pastor told him he could not continue the meeting and asked him to leave. He only had a one-way ticket and was stuck in the city and ran out of money for his hotel.

Note: Please do not travel with a one-way ticket unless you plan to make the city of your destination your new home.

As I listened to his voice on the phone it did not take much discernment to find out why the pastor had cut the meeting short. This visiting minister was an angry young man and was manifesting that spirit to the congregation. Pray for wisdom and patience, and for God to give you the grace to wait for His appointed time for the message to come forth.

CHAPTER 15

TRAVELING MINISTRIES

Women traveling alone should conduct themselves in a godly way. Do not accept invitations from those in the congregation unless approved by the headship of the church. You are not in the meeting to shop and tour the city. This can be done at the proper time.

Do not have everyone running back and forth in your hotel room, especially when traveling alone. It is wise when traveling that others do not know where you are staying. We are living in an hour where we must walk in wisdom.

It is wisdom for the congregation not to know which hotel you are staying in. Only those who are designated to minister to you while you are in the city should have knowledge of your accommodations. Many women over the years have found themselves in positions that have caused some to question their integrity because of the ignorance displayed. If you are still battling with your flesh in certain areas you should stay away from traveling until you have complete victory. The enemy can set you up and ruin your reputation before you know it. Sit at the feet of someone who has experience and allow them to mentor you and speak into your life. Remember, they watch over your soul.

I have experienced certain ones who made attempts to locate where I was staying in a city while I was conducting a meeting. They have come to my hotel, and thank God the person at the desk would not give them my room number. Being a single woman and many times traveling alone, the enemy would attempt to slander my reputation. I would never invite them to my room, but would always come down to the lobby in a public place and discuss whatever was on their mind. Many times I just told the desk clerk I was unavailable at that time, and I would see them at the meeting. If it was anything of importance, I would meet with them in the office of the church in the presence of the pastor. I have made a practice of never counseling with a church member unless it has been by the request of the pastor.

In the past I have seen many traveling ministries contact church members for finances, relationships, and you name it. This is not appropriate and if you have been guilty of doing this, I would suggest you refrain because it is unethical and does not show the excellence of character we all should be walking in.

PACKING FOR THE TRIP

There are many changes in air travel today. There was a time we could carry our entire closet and it would not cost us; however, today is a different day. Therefore we must be wise in our selection of clothing for travel. Ladies, we really do not have to carry every shoe and purse to match every dress. We can select one purse that goes with all of our garments. Select clothing that you can roll tightly in your luggage that will not be heavy. Not only will we save money at check-in, but we are also being mindful and respectful to those who must pick us up at the airport.

If two or more are traveling, many times the person picking up the passenger has to rent a van just for the luggage, and we never even wear everything we have brought.

LEAVING A TIP

I have traveled with some who have not been gracious in tipping the bellboy or the taxi driver, yet they have two and three pieces of luggage. If you want to demonstrate a Christlike spirit, always leave a tip for the maid that takes care of your room and does the little extra favors for you. They will look forward to your return and do even more for you.

At the airport

The first opportunity to tip during travel is usually upon arriving at the airport or train station. Here are some tipping guidelines:

- Porter or skycap: $2.00 per bag or more if the bags are heavy. $2.00 extra for curbside check-in is optional at some airports. If you arrive late and he helps you get to your flight on time, tip an extra $5.00–$20.00 (at many of the airports it is mandatory, $2.00 a bag).

- Electric cart driver: $2.00–$3.00 a person.

- Wheelchair pusher: If they are just pushing you down the ramp from the gate to the plane (or in reverse), then nothing. If it is from the ticket counter to the gate/plane or from the gate/plane to the luggage carousel, then $5.00 is appropriate. Tip more if they help you with your luggage ($1.00–$2.00 per bag) or if they help you to your car. If they are pushing you from one terminal to another (long distances), then $10.00–$20.00 would be appropriate plus extra for luggage. Tip less if they are unpleasant or rude.

Ground transportation

- Taxi, limo, paid shuttle, or van driver: 15 percent of the total fare. Up to 20 percent if the driver helps with the bags or makes extra stops. No less than $1.00. If someone else is picking up the tab, they are responsible for tipping also. Be careful, the rate quoted for limos often includes gratuity.

- Driver of courtesy shuttle: $1.00–$2.00 per bag if he helps with the bags.

- Auto dealership shuttle driver: Nothing.

At the hotel

Before you arrive at a nicer hotel or resort, inquire as to whether gratuities are included in the price of the room. Some hotels are now charging a daily fee that covers all tipping for hotel services. If there is not a daily fee, these rates are appropriate:

- Valet or parking attendant: $1.00–$3.00 is appropriate for parking or returning the car. It is not necessary to tip for parking, but always for returning the car.

- Doorman: If he hails you a cab, $1.00–$2.00. If he helps you with your bags in or out of the car, $1.00 a bag. Use $1.00–$2.00 per bag if he carries them all the way to the room. If he just opens the door, nothing. If he is helpful with directions or restaurant recommendations, $5.00.

- Bellman: When he helps you with your bags, tip $1.00–$2.00 per bag. Give him the tip when he shows you your room. If he just carries the bags to the front desk and then disappears, save it for the person who carries the bags to your room. Upon checkout, tip a bellman who helps with your bags. Tip more for additional services.

- Front desk: Typically there is no tip for the front desk, but if they help you with early check-in or late check-out, tip $1.00–$2.00.

- Concierge: $5.00–$10.00 for help with hard-to-get dinner reservations or theater tickets. Tipping is optional for just plain advice, but $5.00 is the minimum. Tipping can be done at the end of the trip or at the time of service, just keep it straight so that you are fair.

- Butler: $5.00–$10.00 per service or $50.00–$100.00 per night. Very special services like meals when the restaurant is closed are more like $50.00.

- Room service: If gratuity is included, add nothing or $1.00. Otherwise add 15–20 percent of the total charge.

- Delivery of special items: If you request extra pillows or an iron, tip $1.00 per item received, minimum $2.00.

- Maid service: $3.00–$5.00 per day typically, up to $10.00 per day depending upon how much mess you make. Tip daily because there might be a different maid each day. Leave the tip on your pillow, and tip on the last day also. If they change out your linens by request, give $1.00–$2.00 each time.

You can look online for further information on etiquette in tipping.

TIPS WHEN INVITED TO HOMES

Ladies, when you are invited to someone's home, it is nice to take a hostess gift, especially when invited to a meal. I realize many courtesies have changed over the years; however, this is thoughtful. It does not have to be expensive, just a small bouquet of flowers, or fruit. If you give a present as a hostess gift and it is wrapped, do not expect the hostess to open it right away. She will open it more than likely when all of her guests are gone.

This saves the embarrassment of others who might not have brought a gift, or maybe it is something you do not want to share.

CHAPTER 16

DINNER PARTY ETIQUETTE—WHAT YOU SHOULD KNOW

THERE HAVE BEEN many changes in etiquette at dinner parties. Years ago the dos and don'ts were written in stone. Yes, there have been many changes; however, I still believe there are some guidelines we can be aware of and choose whether to follow them or not. I have listed those questions that are frequently asked.

How long should you wait for overdue guests? Usually there will be about half an hour to an hour between arrival and dinner. If a guest still hasn't arrived, there is no need to delay dinner more than fifteen minutes unless you wish, and the dinner won't be spoiled. But not much longer, your other guests deserve to be fed on time.

When the latecomers arrive, just invite them to join you at the table at whatever course you are on. There is no need to rush out to the kitchen and get them a first course if everyone is on the main course.

It may be considered fashionable to arrive late in Hollywood, but at a dinner party this is considered bad etiquette. The last thing you want is to hold up the meal while everyone waits on your arrival. If you must show up late, do your best to arrive no more than thirty minutes past the time indicated on your invitation. It is very good manners to call your hostess and make her aware of your situation.

Please do not arrive an hour early. The hostess has to entertain you while doing last-minute details.

Only bring a guest if the invitation requests you do so. If you did not RSVP for a guest, it's very bad manners to show up with one in tow. The menu has already been planned and the table has been set. An uninvited guest would cause a disruption as your hostess shuffles to make a place at the table and rearrange food on dinner plates.

INTRODUCING GUESTS

If you have invited people who don't know everyone, plan ahead for an introduction that leaves guests a "conversational book" to let them start chatting. For example: "This is John, he has just moved to our neighborhood this year."

Don't place things on the table like keys, purses, or other items. Tuck them under your chair if you need them nearby. Guests, please turn off your cell phones.

USING THE TABLEWARE

For using the dishes, remember the rule, "Eat from the left, drink from the right." That means your bread plate or salad plate will be the one on your left.

Don't be intimidated by the vast array of silverware surrounding your plates. If you're unsure of the order in which to use your silverware, a good rule of thumb is to work your way in from the outside. If you're still uncertain, follow the lead of those around you. It is good to remember that dirty silverware should never touch the tablecloth.

DINNER PARTY EATING ETIQUETTE

Unless told otherwise, wait until everyone is seated and served before starting to eat. Often a host or hostess will tell people to go ahead; in this case, feel free to do so.

Try to pace your eating so that you don't race to the finish line before others are halfway through. If you are a slow eater, try to speed up a bit so you don't hold everyone up.

Do not talk with food in your mouth; just wait until you have swallowed your food, then answer. It's customary to break your roll into pieces and butter rather than to cut and butter all at once.

Did your mother always tell you to keep your elbows off the table? Well, try to keep them off when you are eating. It's not so important these days when you are just talking.

Unfold your napkin and place it on your lap. When you are finished, place it loosely on the table, not on the plate. Don't get upset if you spill something. Accidents happen, and this is a dinner party with friends. Just fix it and don't keep on apologizing.

After each course, your hostess, or someone hired for this purpose, will clear the table. A good hostess will never let her guests stare at dirty dishes while waiting for the next course to arrive.

After the main course is finished, all the dishes and condiments for that course should be removed. This includes salt and pepper and butter. After dessert, dishes may stay on the table while the company talks together and drinks coffee or tea.

If you are invited to a dinner do not ask for leftovers to take home.

When you are ready to leave, do not hold the hostess at the open door talking all night.

Three days to one week after the event, call or send your hostess a note thanking her for the lovely evening.

CHAPTER 17

ETIQUETTE ON THE CELL PHONE

Turn your cell phone ringer off. If you have your cell phone at work, it shouldn't ring. If you don't want to turn off your cell phone completely, at least set it to vibrate. The sounds of different ringtones going off all the time can be very annoying to others.

Let your cell phone calls go to voice mail. While you are at work, if you are in doubt about whether an incoming call is important, let voice mail pick it up. It will take much less time to check your messages than it will to answer the call and then tell the caller you can't talk.

Find a private place to make cell phone calls. While it's OK to use your cell phone at work for private calls during breaks, don't stay at your desk. Find somewhere else to talk where your conversation can't be overheard, even if what you're discussing isn't personal. You may be on a break but your co-workers have a job to do.

Don't bring your cell phone into the restroom... ever. This rule should apply to using your cell phone at work or anywhere. You never know who's in there; the person on the other end of the line will hear bathroom sounds, e.g., toilets flushing; it is an invasion of your co-workers' privacy.

Don't bring your cell phone to meetings. Even if you have your cell phone set to vibrate, if you receive a call you will be tempted to see who it's from. This is not only rude; it is a clear signal to the person speaking that your mind isn't 100 percent on the meeting. All calls can wait until your meeting is over or until there is a break. Remember, there was a time when we didn't have cell phones and we managed well.

Don't talk too loudly. For some reason people feel the need to raise their voices while on their phones. I think we've come far enough, technologically speaking, to trust the phone's microphone to adequately amplify and carry your voice.

Don't hold inappropriate conversations in public. Keep your personal conversations personal. Offer to call the person back, step outside, or find a quiet place where you can speak more freely.

I see ministries constantly using their cell phones in church during service; unless it is an emergency this is rude.

The other day I was in line at the supermarket and the whole line had to wait for the person who was at the counter to finish their conversation before the clerk could finish serving them. This was not respectful to the clerk as well as those who had to wait until the person finished their business on the phone.

It is annoying to be speaking with someone and they are constantly getting calls on their phone.

TEXTING WHILE DRIVING

Many states have banned the use of cell phones while driving due to the many accidents that have taken place.

According to the US National Safety Council, every year 1.6 million accidents are caused by cell phone use. Of these 1.6 million accidents, 1.4 million are caused by talking on the phone while driving, while at least 200,000 of these accidents are caused by texting while driving.[1]

These guidelines for the cell phone do not apply to women only but to everyone who has access to a cell phone.

I pray that these guidelines will be just that—guidelines to help you be all that God has called you to be.

NOTES

CHAPTER 2

1. *Compton's Interactive Encyclopedia* (Compton's NewMedia, Inc., 1995).
2. Ibid.
3. Ibid.
4. Ibid.
5. Ibid.
6. Ibid.
7. Ibid.
8. Ibid.
9. Ibid.
10. Ibid.
11. Ibid.
12. Ibid.
13. Ibid.

14. "Women in the Labor Force in 2010," United States Department of Labor, Women's Bureau, http://www.dol.gov/wb/factsheets/Qf-laborforce-10.htm (accessed September 7, 2012).

CHAPTER 6

1. Sarah Dowdey, "How Smells Work," *How Stuff Works*, http://science.howstuffworks.com/environmental/life/human-biology/smell.htm (accessed September 6, 2012).

CHAPTER 10

1. Susan Bixler and Nancy Nix-Rice, *The New Professional Image*, 2nd ed. (Avon, MA: Adams Media, 2005), 3.

2. Stephen Boyd, "Appearance Is Important," *Public Speaking Tips*, 2009, http://www.speaking-tips.com/Articles/Appearance-Is-Important.aspx (accessed September 7, 2012).

CHAPTER 11

1. Wikipedia: The Free Encyclopedia, s.v. "Salt in the Bible," http://en.wikipedia.org/wiki/Salt_in_the_Bible (accessed September 7, 2012).

CHAPTER 13

1. From website: http://EzineArticles.com/?expert=Gilles_CoulombeArticle, http://EzineArticles.com/1381972 (accessed September 10, 2012).

CHAPTER 17

1. US National Safety Council, 2010, http://www.nsc.org/Pages/NSCestimates16million crashescausedbydriversusingcellphonesandtexting.aspx (accessed September 7, 2012).

ABOUT THE AUTHOR

Apostle Delores L. Kendrick is senior pastor and founder of Tabernacle of Praise Church in Seattle, Washington. Apostle Kendrick has served in ministry for more than thirty years. She has been called for this season to equip the saints (Eph. 4) in higher dimensions of spiritual warfare, which prepares them for kingdom living and kingdom service. Her prophetic voice is known internationally and nationally, where she has declared the works of the Lord by lifting up the body of Christ and preparing them for present truth, and releasing the power of God within the body of Christ through the fivefold ministry!

CONTACT THE AUTHOR

dl.kendrick@att.net